LOST WEEK

A History of Newcastle's Public Houses

~Volume Three~

The West

Brian Bennison

Newcastle Libraries & Information Service

Acknowledgements:

As ever, I am indebted to the City Library's Local Studies Section and Tyne & Wear Archives. I must also thank Laura Bennison, Jimmy Donald, Jimmy Forsyth, Ken Foxon, Chris Goulding, Lynn Pearson and Des Walton. Anna Flowers deserves all the credit for the appearance of the final product.

Photographic acknowledgements:

All photographs are copyright of Newcastle Libraries & Information Service except for the following reproduced courtesy of:
Jimmy Forsyth: front cover and pages 7, 19, 20, 24;
Northern Echo: page 46;
Stagecoach Busways: page 18;
Tyne & Wear Archives: back cover and pages 8, 11, 12, 16, 23, 26, 33, 34, 36;
West Newcastle Local Studies: page 38.

Front cover: Mr Ferguson cleans the windows at the Green Tree, Laurel St, Scotswood in 1958.

Back cover: The George the First, George St in the late 1940s.

Cover design by A.V. Flowers.

Also by Brian Bennison and published by Newcastle Libraries & Information Service:

Heady Days – a History of Newcastle's Public Houses: Volume One the Central Area, 1996.

Heavy Nights – a History of Newcastle's Public Houses: Volume Two the North and East, 1997.

Brewers and Bottlers of Newcastle upon Tyne, 1995.

Photographs which are copyright of Newcastle Libraries & Information Service may be ordered and purchased from the Local Studies Section, Newcastle City Library.

For a free catalogue of our local history publications write to:

Publications
City Library
Princess Square
Newcastle Upon Tyne
NE99 1DX

Or telephone 0191 2610691

Printed by Bailes the Printer, Houghton le Spring

Contents

Photographs

Children, one barefooted, gather outside the Stanhope House when Margaret Cunningham was the licensee in 1906.

1

Arthur's Hill

New Mills, an area to the west of Barrack Rd where two windmills were sited, was served in the mid-19th century by the **Barrack Tavern** beerhouse. It became the **Darnell House** (later the **Darnell Hotel**) on rebuilding in 1892. The new name reflected the influence on the area of a wealthy cleric, W N Darnell, Rector of Stanhope, who by the 1840s owned a tract of land between Barrack Rd and Westgate Rd. The premises were bought by North Eastern Breweries in 1897 and in 1935 became a fully-fledged public house when the **Hope & Anchor**, Horatio St, closed and its licence transferred. In 1937 the owners acquired 5000 square yards of adjoining land on which they proposed to build two bowling rinks and a car park, but the brewery was refused permission to construct an indoor bowling-rink, which would have been only the second in Britain after Cheltenham. As a Vaux house, the **Darnell** re-emerged in 1995 as the **Old Mill**, became the **New Darnell** and was demolished with the adjoining Todd's Nook School in 1998.

Higginbottom's **Windsor Castle**, referred to by locals as the 'Barrel', disappeared from Barrack Rd in 1908. Until 1888 it had been the **Sir John Moore**, after the British general killed by Napoleonic troops in Spain and whose funeral was celebrated in the poem, *The Burial of Sir John Moore at Corunna*. In 1870 the pub went on sale as the **General Moore**, said to adjoin the Ponteland Turnpike and have a four-roomed cottage in its yard. On the corner of Barrack Rd and Stanhope St stands the **Black Bull** (once the **Old Black Bull**), part of the Haymarket Brewery's estate taken over by Newcastle Breweries in 1896 and rebuilt in 1938.

A new public house stands on the eastern side of Barrack Rd, although the building itself has much historical significance. In 1804, during the Napoleonic emergency, the Incorporated Companies of Newcastle agreed to rent out part of the Town Moor to allow the construction of Fenham Barracks. Two gatehouses, thought to be by celebrated architect James Wyatt, were added in 1816. When the barracks were eventually vacated by the army, the gatehouses became the property of the City Council which sought to knock them down

A small outbreak of fire at the Darnell Hotel, Barrack Rd, January 22 1932.

in the early 1980s. Following a public inquiry, the Dept of the Environment refused the council permission to demolish, arguing that this rare example of military architecture was 'an historical monument to almost two centuries of association between the people of Newcastle and the many regiments which have passed through the gates during its development from a frontier garrison town to a great city'. Various unsuccessful attempts were made to utilise the gatehouses before it was announced that they were to be 'converted into Tyneside's latest swish eating and drinking spot'. The **Inn on the Park** opened in 1986, became the **Cushy Billet** in 1995 and was relaunched as the **Leazes Inn** in 1998.

On the corner of Barrack Rd and Pitt St the **Lord Hill** (previously the **Hound Inn**) closed in 1966 to be replaced by the **Magpie** and the Blue Star Club. The site is now used for carparking. The **Lord Hill** was the first changing-room for St James' Park: when Newcastle West End began to play on the land that would develop into St James' Park they stripped in the **Lord Hill**, where the licensee was a member of the football club's board. Spectators readily attributed a poor performance by the team to the fact that the players had visited the pub to do more than change for the game. Jokes about certain players taking to the field drunk assumed the status of legend. One story told of a defender who started the match in splendid form with several beautifully judged clearances, supposedly turned to a team-mate and asked: 'Which way we kickin'?'.

In Stanhope St, on the corner of Spring St, stood the **Lord Harding**, which closed in 1910 and was known by its customers as the 'Bob the Noddin'. Also in Stanhope St, the **Stanhope** beerhouse in Croydon Rd became a spirit merchant's shop around 1910. In Campbell St the tiny, one-roomed **Campbell House** was closed in 1921. The **Mitre** closed at the beginning of the 1920s. An early closure in Spring St, in 1884, had been the **Prince George** beerhouse (once called the **Prince George of Cambridge**). In Hill St Robt Deuchar bought the **Boilermakers'**

Arms in 1897 and the **Footballers' Arms** (once the **Footballers' Rest**) twelve months later.

The **Boilermakers' Arms** closed in 1910 but the **Footballers' Arms**, rebuilt in 1899, stayed open until 1939.

At the junction of Arbinger St and Diana St the **Tankerville Arms** closed in 1909. Also in Diana St, the **Eagle Tavern closed** in 1938 when its licence was transferred to the **Fosse** on Roman Avenue. On the corner of Diana St and Douglas Terrace the **Travellers' Rest** was renamed the **King's Arms**, probably on rebuilding in 1878. In 1892 the ground floor of the building had 'a bar divided into a general bar and bottle & jug department, and a small sitting room from which a cellar has been partitioned'. It was being rented by a Mrs Davison for £130 per annum. It closed in the late 1980s, but was reopened by the Legendary Yorkshire Heroes company in 1990. Despite the words **King's Arms** being prominent in the brickwork of the public house, its name was changed in quick succession to **O'Dwyer's**, the **Cuckoo** (a 19th century nickname) and the **Magpie** in 1994. It now stands boarded up awaiting a buyer.

In Pitt St the **Plough** ceased trading in 1907, whilst the **Hare Inn** and the **Oddfellows Arms** both closed one year later. The **Greyhound** still stands after being rebuilt in in 1899, changing hands for £6,900 in 1920, becoming a Bass house in 1958 and then auctioned off by the company in 1982. It was bought by Jennings Bros of Cockermouth, and renamed the **Cumberland Wrestler**. It has been known as the **Milburn** since 1990. The **Plumbers Arms**, with entrances on both Pitt St and Wellington St, was 'a well-frequented public house' before its closure in 1910.

In Wellington St the **Wellington Arms** beerhouse closed in 1881 when its owner-landlord was judged to be an 'unsatisfactory character'; the **Joiners' Arms** lost its licence in 1908; and the **Foresters Arms** closed in 1910 to become a shop. The **Duke of Wellington** closed in 1909 and was converted to the Newcastle upon Tyne Amalgamated Musicians' Union

The former Prince of Wales in 1956. The pub closed before the Second World War when the area was the subject of a compulsory purchase order on slum clearance, but the building remained until work began on the Hill St flats.

Working Men's Club, which quickly became the Novo Castria Social Club and continued at that address until 1980 when new premises were erected in Stanhope St. Also in Wellington St, the **Prince of Wales** was bought by Barras & Co for £1,110 in 1883, became a Newcastle Breweries house in 1890 and was rebuilt in 1907. The pub is remembered for its marble-fronted bar and Prince of Wales plumes in the elegant exterior tilework. It closed in 1938 and the licence transferred to a new **Prince of Wales** at the corner of Westgate Rd and Lewis Drive, which was opened in 1939. A refurbishment of 1982 completely transformed the ground floor of the new **Prince of Wales** . This was necessary, said the owners, because 'the Prince was a typical pub of 1930s vintage which was designed when licensed premises were male preserves, with lots of smallish rooms.

The Duke of Edinburgh c.1950. Older people knew the pub as the 'Red Lamp', an allusion to a less than respectable feature of its past.

Today, ladies play an equally important part on the pub scene and they demand a nicer atmosphere'.

In Seaham St the **Seaham Tavern** closed in 1908. The **Hodgson's Arms** survived until 1995. At the turn of the century it had a bar and two sitting rooms, with a side entrance in Oakes Place and a back door in Pitt Lane. It had been on the brink of closure in 1937, but it was allowed to keep open on condition that it was modernised.

On the corner of Douglas Terrace and Church St (later renamed Avison St after a distinguished Newcastle composer), the **Merry Monarch** (a sobriquet applied to Charles II) was a beerhouse. It graduated to a public house in 1879 with a licence transferred from the **Steamboat** in St Mary's St and closed in

1969. Also in Douglas Terrace, the **Earl of Douglas** was bought by the Pine Street Brewery in 1892, was altered in 1907, again during the 1930s and then in 1944 when a club room was opened on the first floor. It was bought by Hope & Anchor Breweries for £4,000 in 1954 and closed in 1970.

In Moor St the **Duke of Edinburgh** was taken over by Robt Deuchar in 1897. At that time the public house had a large bar with dividing partitions, a smoke room and a bottle and jug department on the ground floor. Upstairs there was a sitting room and a billiards room with two tables. The **Duke of Edinburgh** was rebuilt in 1937 and demolished in 1994.

Two small pubs in Edward St – the **Smiths' Arms** and the **Lord Raglan** – lost their licences in 1881. In Cottenham St the **White Lion** (formerly the **Pickwick Inn** with 'clay ends' in its yard) closed in 1909 and the **Prince Consort** in 1911. On the corner of Mansfield St and Bayley St the **Heather Bell** closed in 1910, as did the small, stone-built **Northumberland Arms** in William St.

2

Westgate

Westgate's concentration of licensed premises in a small area often earned it the unenviable annual accolade as the city's top district for drunkenness: in 1897, for example, there were 1,322 prosecutions. Many pubs brewed their own beer, including the **Saddlers' Wells Inn** and the **Elephant & Castle** in Low Friar St. A dispensary had been converted to 'a place of entertainment' (a music hall, art gallery etc) in 1840 and then modified to function as the **Saddlers' Wells Inn** until it lost its licence in 1892. The **Elephant & Castle**, a popular miners' pub in the 19th century, closed in 1935.

The **Bakers' & Brewers' Arms** stood in Stowell Square, its name commemorating one of Newcastle's ancient guilds. Recognised in a charter from Edward III in 1341, the Bakers and Brewers of Newcastle were later granted the exclusive right to provide bread and ale for the whole of the Port of Tyne. The Guild subsequently conducted its affairs according to rules drawn up in 1661, including the proviso that 'every brother was to behave decently and quietly at meetings' and was forbidden to 'strike another with fist, hand, elbow, dagger, staff, stick, rod or otherwise, on pain of twenty shillings'. The Guild had premises in Blackfriars and the **Bakers' & Brewers' Arms** was opened in property it owned in Stowell Square around 1828. The pub was eventually acquired by the Grey Horse Brewery in Gallowgate and then by the Northumberland Public House Trust before closing in 1917. In Stowell St the **Sir William Wallace Arms** and the **Burton House**, two small premises with beer-only licences, shut up shop during the First World War.

The **Brandy Vaults**, on the corner of Waterloo St and Westgate Rd, closed in 1963 and became the Garden City Chinese restaurant. Next door, the **Crown** was rebuilt in 1860 and in 1896 became the **Crown Buffet**, before graduating via the **Stoll Theatre Buffet** and the **Tyne Theatre Buffet** to the **Pit Bar**. The licence appears to have been used to re-open the **Brandy Vaults**, which closed briefly and then re-opened again as **Tilley's** in 1991, incorporating more of the old **Tyne Buffet**. The choice of name and general theatrical theme was determined by the emerging redevelopment of the area under the Theatre Village banner. Across the road, the **Waterloo Inn was** owned from 1897 by wine and spirit merchants, MacFadyen & Co., who had a number of public houses in the west end of the city. In those days it consisted of a bar with four entrances and sitting accommodation on the ground floor, along with a club room upstairs. It came into the hands of Hammond's of Bradford in 1962 and was held by Bass until its licence was surrendered in 1992 to enable the brewers to launch the **Akenside Traders** on the Side. In 1998 the Newcastle Foyer, managed by the Salvation Army Housing Association, opened on the site.

The **Pineapple** in Westgate Rd had been rebuilt in 1862 but closed at the turn of the century when the Pavillion Theatre was erected. The adjoining **Black Bull** was once owned by Jacob Wilkinson who brewed in a three storey building at the rear, but the brewery collapsed when the foundations of the Pavillion

Westgate Rd in the early years of the century when electric trams were running, but before the Pavilion was built. In the centre of the picture stands the Pine Apple, with its name just visible on the white lamp, and the Black Bull to its left. The picture may have been taken during ceremonies marking the end of the Boer War in June 1902.

were being dug. On Wilkinson's death the **Black Bull** was put up for auction, and withdrawn when bidding reached £8,600, but private negotiations led to its purchase by John Fitzgerald. It closed in 1992 but was re-opened in 1995 as the **Bodega**, a title by which many customers had referred to part of it in the past. The owners exercised care in preserving the old pub's best features, particularly the two stained-glass domes in the ceiling.

BLACK BULL INN,

(Next door to this Theatre).

THEATRICALS SPECIALLY CATERED FOR.
PROP. · JACOB WILKINSON

Everything of the Finest Quality.

—

WINES, SPIRITS, & CIGARS.

—

HOME BREWED MILD ALES.

The Black Bull advertises its specialities in 1905.

The **Carlisle**, on the corner of Westgate Rd and Blenheim St, was acquired by Robt Deuchar in 1897, transferred to Newcastle Breweries in the 1950s, and closed in 1965. The building that was once the **Carlisle** stills stands; a proposal has been mooted which would use the Hodgson's **Arms** licence to re-open the old **Carlisle** as a bar and restaurant within the Theatre Village scheme.

The **William IV**, known as the 'Halfway House', closed in 1972. The frequent use of William IV's name for licensed premises was due to his claim to be remembered as the monarch that lowered the tax on beer. The former **William IV now** operates as Charlie's computer games shop and although remodelled internally, the stonework of the old pub's door surrounds and the leaded lights above the central entrance clearly indicate the exterior of a familiar style of corner pub of the third quarter of the 19th century, in this case sitting where Westgate Rd and Swinburne Place meet.

The **Bay Horse** on the corner of Westgate Rd and Buckingham St was bought by Robt Deuchar in 1886 and rebuilt at the outbreak of World War Two. It closed in 1993. Also on Westgate Rd the **Gloucester House** closed in 1888 and the **Boar's Head**, which in 1836 advertised 'the cheapest ale in

Newcastle', was rebuilt in 1862 and closed in 1893. The **Times**, erected in 1851, also closed in 1893. It had been built on what was the top of Cumberland Row facing Elswick Lane, and was bought by the Corporation for road-widening. Some of the land was acquired by Wesleyans to establish a mission hall which also served as a centre for Good Templars. The **Times** was the subject of a story about a terrific thunderstorm when lightning struck the top of Westgate Hill and crashed into the pub. As late as 1913 locals were writing to the press passing on tales of how 'several of the Times' inmates were killed'. However, a survey of local newspapers around the time when such dramatic events were believed to have occurred reveals no reports of the fatal bolt from the blue. The 'great storm' appears to be a myth.

The **Talbot** and the **Cookson's Arms** (commemorating Isaac Cookson who owned the estate which, in the 1820s, he named Arthur's Hill after his son) both closed in 1910. The **Goat**, on the corner of Westgate Rd and Bell St, was rebuilt c.1900 and closed

The Carlisle in the early 1950s, surrounded by buildings of the John Sinclair Tobacco Co. which have recently been converted into housing. The Carlisle is still recognisable today, albeit in an unsightly and dilapidated state and partially hidden by hoardings.

The Mill Inn at Christmas 1951. As austerity comes to an end, drinkers can ignore the pub and partake of some of the delights advertised alongside: Max Bygraves playing Buttons at the Empire, new Rowntree's which had 'changed people's ideas about cocoa' and a range of carcinogenic products available at the Mill Newsagency.

Mechanics' Arms was described at the beginning of the century as having 'a well-appointed commodious bar, bar parlour, two splendid cellars and one large tea or sitting room'. It was said to be doing 'lucrative business', being 'close to the cooperative store's new buildings and a large tobacco factory'. The pub lost its licence in 1921.

In Blenheim St the **Alnwick Castle**, described in 1827 as 'a property of attractive character', and bought by Allsopp's in 1898, ceased trading in 1939. The **Locomotive Inn**, a Richard Charlton house from 1873, was sold to the Corporation in 1963 and closed in 1968. Two other Blenheim St pubs survived until 1997 when work began on the West Central road scheme: the **Coach & Horses** (sometimes **Charlton's Coach & Horses**), rebuilt on the corner of Churchill St in 1903 and becoming the **Broken Doll** in 1983; and the **Queen Victoria**, altered in the 1920s, becoming the **Black & White** in 1981 and **Strings** in 1988. In 1961 the **Queen Victoria**'s manageress was Florence Morley, a lady in her seventies. One morning, shortly before she was to retire, she was working in the cellar oblivious to the fact that smoke was billowing from upstairs windows. When she answered the frantic banging on her door she found an apologetic passer-by saying 'I'm sorry to bother you pet, but do you know your pub's on fire?'

In Blandford St the **Blandford Arms** closed in 1880. The **Lord Palmerston** (formerly the **Palmerston**) closed in 1922

in 1965; as did the nearby **Masons' Arms**, bought by Fitzgerald's in 1884. The **Balmoral**, on the corner of what was Worley St, was bought by Fitzgerald's in 1892 and still stands. Also surviving is the **Mill Inn**, originally at Elswick Mill (becoming part of Westgate Rd in 1893). It became Newcastle's most expensive beerhouse, a record £3,500 having been paid for it at auction in 1897. It came near to closure in 1901 when the justices refused to renew its licence because it was 'a house of disorderly character', although it survived on appeal.

Four public houses closed in 1915: the **Britannia** and the **Nightingale Tavern** in Churchill St, the **Fountain Inn** in Lord St and the **Duke of Cambridge** in Duke St. In Temple St the

when magistrates refused to renew its licence after considering the number and condition of licensed houses in the Westgate Rd area. Two other pubs – the **Lord Clyde** and the **Mechanics' Arms** – also lost their licences, along with five beerhouses. The **Marquis of Blandford**, on the corner of Blandford St and Westgate Rd, had originally belonged to the Hanover Street Brewery, was bought by Jas Deuchar in 1925 for £7,650 and was owned by Newcastle Breweries on its closure in 1971.

In Sunderland St the **Bridge Inn** (once the **Sunderland Bridge Inn**) had its licence rescinded in 1893 when 'frequented by prostitutes'. Along the same street, the **Volunteer Arms** was closed in 1906 when 'ill-conducted and frequented by bad characters'. It prompted the following comment:

'No more of service to City or Crown
The Volunteer Arms are at last laid down'.

There were three public houses in Thornton St until the last quarter of the 19th century: the **Falstaff Hotel** traded until 1875, the **Alnwick House** closed in 1883 and the **Clarendon Hotel** lost its licence in 1891 when 'frequented by thieves, prostitutes and persons of bad character'. In Villa Place the **Beehive Inn** was sold by Newcastle Breweries to the Newcastle Housing Improvement Trust in the mid-1920s and demolished. In Bath Lane the **Tyne Brewery** public house was built in 1868 when the Tyne Brewery Co. erected its new Tyne Brewery. When the company failed its houses passed via Wm Younger's to W B Reid, whilst the brewery became the headquarters of Newcastle Breweries. Reid's therefore changed the name of the public house to the **King Brewery** and eventually, in 1921, a swap was arranged whereby Newcastle Breweries took possession of the **King Edward** and Reid's acquired the Dock Inn at North Shields. The **King Edward** survived until 1952 when its licence was transferred to the **Rokeby**, Stamfordham Rd.

In Corporation Street the **Bath Hotel closed** in 1966. Ken Foxon, who celebrated his 'twenty-first' in the pub in Coronation Year, remembers his local as 'a typical street corner pub with a bar running from the corner of Bath Lane Terrace down Corporation St, another little bar, but a very smart function room upstairs'.

In Buckingham St the **Lord Lyons** closed in 1908 and the **Royal Burton House** followed in 1909. Operating on a beer-only licence, the **Royal Burton House** consisted of a bar, tap-room and clubroom above. Part of the same property was a large shop which at the turn of the century was let as a mission hall. The **Duke of Buckingham** had a bar, bar parlour and snug when it was sold for £2,060 in 1893. In 1922 it was bought by Scottish brewers Calder's along with two pubs in South Shields for £15,000, but the **Duke of Buckingham** could not escape the slum clearance of 1937. The **Clock**, a Jas Deuchar pub from 1884 until the 1950s takeover by Newcastle Breweries, was altered in 1921 and rebuilt c.1938 in the white-fronted style popular with breweries at that time. It closed in 1975.

Among the pubs to disappear from Oyster Shell Lane were the **Oystershell Inn** in 1883 when 'dilapidated and unfit', the **Fountain Inn** in 1891 and the **Bricklayers' Arms** in 1895. The **Hedley Arms**, on the corner of Oyster Shell Lane and Hedley St, was bought by J H Graham in 1874. He rebuilt the adjoining brewery in 1886 and although the public house closed in 1908, the Hedley Street Brewery continued and became the first Federation Brewery in 1921. In Hedley Place the **Northumberland Arms** closed in 1908.

An early loss from Waterloo St was the **Uncle Tom's Cabin** beerhouse in 1874. Two other long-gone public houses are the **Black Bull Inn** and the **Lord Clyde**. When it changed hands in 1894, the Black **Bull** had a bar, smoke room, snug, sitting room, clubroom and thirteen bedrooms. It closed in 1914 with Charlton's Bonds being built on the site. The **Lord Clyde** had its licence removed by magistrates in 1922. The old **Wheatsheaf** almost closed during the Second World War but the licensing justices reprieved it when improvements were made. The pub

The Wheatsheaf Inn in 1893. Mrs P. Greenland, landlady, advertises Sir Augustus Harris's Royal Italian Opera Co., fresh from a performance at Windsor Castle, playing at the nearby Tyne Theatre. A bull is driven up Waterloo Street away from the cattle market.

Anderson, and suggested they go together 'to view the Great Fire raging in Gateshead'. Anderson began to get dressed to go but realised he had work to do in the pub and anyway, 'thought he has seen so many fires, he would not bother with this one'. Sharp's curiosity got the better of him and he went ahead. He was last seen on Davidson's gangway before perishing like so many others on that fateful day.

Westmorland St lost the **General Wolsley Inn** in 1901 and the **Grey Bull** in 1919. The **Westmorland** (sometimes the **Westmorland Arms** and later the **Earl of Westmorland**) changed hands in 1920 for £2,500, became a McEwan's house in the early 1950s and transferred its licence to the newly-built **Balloon** in Silver Lonnen. The **White Bull**, on the corner of Westmorland St and Marlborough Crescent, became **Olley's Bar** in 1983 and then the **Barking Dog** in 1989.

Four public houses have disappeared from Marlborough Crescent: the original **Shepherd's Inn** (later the **Flowers' Inn**, the **Argyle House** and the **Rising Sun**) in 1905, the **Marlborough House** (formerly the **Belford House**) which let its licence lapse in 1913, the **Woolpack** which shut up shop in 1915 and the **Earl of Durham** which also closed in 1915 and was converted to a factory. In the 1890s the **Argyle House** had been described as 'among the handsomest in the city. The rooms consist of a downstairs public bar, adjoining which is a

survives but has undergone the seemingly inevitable name-change for this part of the city and is now the **Frog & Nightgown** after a number of years as the **Paddock**. One morning in 1854, Thos Sharp, a 'retired gentleman', called upon the landlord of what was then the **Wheat Sheaf Inn**, Mr J

smartly upholstered snug for better-class customers. Upstairs is a billiard room, a large and well lighted apartment with its attendant bar. It is unmistakeably one of the most attractive billiard rooms in these parts. With a first-class billiard table, the latest appurtenances, convenient and even luxuriant side seating, and the walls finely decorated with well executed pictures, it is no wonder that it is a favourite rendezvous for habitues of the cue.'

At the bottom of Scotswood Rd and the corner of Churchill St stands the old **King's Head** (once the **King's Head Inn**). When Jas Deuchar acquired it in 1896 it had a large billiard room and both 'select' and 'common' bars. The premises were 'fitted with electric light throughout, with the exception of the common bar'. The **King's Head** became the **Courtyard** in 1983. Now in a rather isolated position, the pub had been very popular with those employed in the meat market which once dominated that part of the town. The **King's Head** enjoyed a reputation amongst butchery workers as a pub for lock-ins and amongst other drinkers as a place to acquire the Sunday joint at cost price. Close by, the **Rokeby Arms** beerhouse closed on the outbreak of the First World War.

Further up Scotswood Road stood the **Graham's Arms** (once **Cook's Hotel**) which in 1900 had three front entrances, a divid-

Graham's Arms Hotel, ———

Bass' and McEwan's Ales only. Guinness' Stout, ... Finest Scotch & Irish Whiskies Wines, Cigars, etc.. all Finest Brands. **Buffet Bar. . . .**

Dinners, . . Luncheons, Chops, Steaks, etc.
SCOTSWOOD ROAD (opposite Cattle Market) **NEWCASTLE - ON - TYNE.** Three minutes walk from Central Station.
Bedrooms Refurnished.
Special Terms for Weekly Boarders.
PROPRIETOR, **J. Pettigrew,** Late of Newburn and Wylam.
Moderate Charges.

The Graham's Arms tempts customers in 1903.

ed long bar and two sitting rooms. There was a covered quoits ground in the rear and the property also accommodated the dining rooms of Ormston's Cattle Market Cafe. The **Graham's Arms** closed in 1908 when said by the owners, North Eastern Breweries, to be doing a respectable trade amongst cattle drovers and farmers attending market. Unfortunately, the tenant had a string of convictions for permitting drunkenness on the premises and refusing to admit the police in the exercise of their duty.

Next door to the **Graham's Arms**, the **Eagle Tavern** was rebuilt in 1891 and later renamed the **Golden Eagle**. It survived until 1970. The **Elswick House**, Scotswood Rd, was leased by Robt Emmerson's Burton Brewery in Sandyford and closed in 1915.

The **Fountain**, bought by Bass for £9,000 in 1920, closed in 1965. The pub, at the bottom of Rye Hill, was close to the old premises of the Peoples' Theatre. Chris Goulding recalls the days when the **Fountain** acted as the thespians' watering hole. 'The clientèle included a number of prominent local characters: the matriarch of a notorious local family and her consort, who sat in their usual corner like a ravaged duke and duchess; migrant labourers who would sit in groups drinking beer by the gallon, sharing a newspaper by rotation along with the spectacles to read it with; and a widow, always dressed in black bombazine, who was the local moneylender and was to end her days brutally murdered.'

Opposite the Cattle Market, the **Farmers' Inn** closed in 1966. The **Farmers' Inn** was one of a number of pubs that applied for music and singing licences in the early 1930s but were granted a licence restricted 'solely for the use of wireless telephonic apparatus'. This was on the advice of the Chief Constable who told the justices that 'with regard to the innovation of music licences in public houses, the police feel that there can be no objection to ordinary wireless programmes' but 'the constant repetition of gramophone records of a jazz order' had a 'tendency to lower the standards'.

A familiar sight at the city end of Scotswood Road. Although it last functioned as a pub in the 1960s, the former Blenheim building survived until approach roads were laid to the new Redheugh Bridge.

The **Blenheim**, on the corner of Blenheim St and Scotswood Rd, was bought by Robt Deuchar for £9,000 in 1946. It closed in 1963. The **Marlborough** survives but became **Rockies Disco Bar** in 1986.

In George St, the **Joiner's Arms** (once the **Drovers' Arms**) closed in 1915. The **George** (for many years the **George the First**) survived until 1951 and the **Crystal Palace**, once boasting its own brewery, closed in the following decade. The **Crystal Palace** had been bought by Jas Deuchar in 1939 (along with the Argyle Hotel, Hebburn) for a total of £18,000 .

3

Elswick

The most unusual public house in Elswick was the **Countess of Coventry**, located on the 30 acre King's Meadows Island in the middle of the Tyne. Named after its one-time owner, Mary Beauclerk, wife of Viscount Deerhurst who became Earl of Coventry in 1811, the pub came into its own in the 19th century when river processions and regattas were popular. Fairs and horse racing also took place on the meadows and the pub did a roaring trade on such occasions, but stayed relatively inactive for the rest of the year. Customers were transported by rowing boat, although at times it was possible to walk across. The landlady kept cows and supplemented her income by delivering milk to Elswick by punt. The pub closed when Kings Meadows Island was sold to the Tyne Commissioners and dredged away between 1874 and 1878.

The majority of Elswick's pubs and beerhouses were along Scotswood Rd and amongst the casualties just after the First World War were the **Shell Inn** in 1916, the **Angel Inn** in 1917, the **President Lincoln** in 1920 and the **Sun Inn** in 1921.

In the 1930s the licensing magistrates, calculating that there was a licensed property for every 80 yards of Scotswood Rd, decided that the 78 licences in the area (which included 54 for consumption on the premises) were excessive and began systematically to reduce the number. The first to go, in 1931, was the **Vulcan**. Leased by W B Reid in 1888 and bought by the company in 1895 for £7,100, it was described as containing on the ground floor 'a most commodious and well arranged bar, with bottle and jug department from Alexander St, commercial room and snug'. On the first floor there was a 'club room, sitting room and five dwelling rooms' with a 'two-stalled stable at the rear'. The **Blast Furnace Inn**, which in 1900 had 'handsomely-appointed general and select bars and two front entrances on Scotswood Rd', stopped serving beer in 1932.

Also closed in 1932 was the **British Lion**, altered in 1902 when magistrates ordered that its upper floors be used solely for domestic purposes. In the 1970s one old resident recalled his great uncle who 'kept the British Lion (afterwards Thompson's Red Stamp Stores). The smelters waited on the doorstep at 6am

The Countess of Coventry, King's Meadows Island, in the 1860s.

Looking westwards along Scotswood Rd on the outbreak of World War One. The British Lion had been altered a decade earlier. Across the street, the Park Road Hotel had been rebuilt in 1899 and was owned by Calvert Graham of wine merchants, Graham & Bradley.

to rush in and have a quick pint and a glass of rum before clocking on at the foundry. The counter was lined with drinks before the bolts were drawn. There was no time to lose.'

Amongst other closures in the 1930s was the **Miners' Arms**, a beerhouse which ceased trading in 1933. The Cameron's-owned **Atlas** was threatened with closure in 1928 but gave an

undertaking to provide proper lavatory accommodation for both sexes and make good all dilapidations. It eventually closed in 1933.

The **Lord Wharncliffe**, on the corner of Scotswood Rd and Wharncliffe St, commemorated the statesman James Archibald Stuart-Wortley-Mackenzie who, to the relief of future painters of pub facias, was made Lord Wharncliffe in 1826. He died in 1845 of 'suppressed gout and apoplexy'. The pub had been extended and improved in the late 1880s, shut up shop in 1933, although plans had been drawn up to rebuild it in 1931. The last Scotswood Rd closure of the decade, just as war was about to be declared, was the **Falcon**. Known by many as the 'Bonny Bird', the pub had a statuette of its namesake over the door .

The pubs of Scotswood Rd went through the Second World War unscathed, despite some near misses. The Vickers-Armstrong factories were an important military target and the city's west end was the focus of a number of German bombing missions. On Maundy Thursday, 1941, over fifty aircraft dropped bombs over the north and west of Newcastle, starting 68 fires, damaging 65 houses and closing the Regal Cinema in Fenham. Around 9.25 pm on Easter Monday a boisterous sing-song was taking place in the upstairs room of the **Gun Hotel** when somebody suddenly raced upstairs and burst into the room crying 'Everyone out … Scotswood Road's on fire'. Not having heard the sirens because of their choral efforts, most customers now thought it best to grab their coats and evacuate the pub, carefully avoiding the incendiary bomb on the front step. The **Gun**'s regulars long remembered the one person who hung back as his fellow customers made a bee-line for the exit; not out of respect for age or gender, but so he could sup up the drinks left by the rest.

When the war ended, the pubs of Scotswood Rd carried on as before and it was not until the late 1950s that closures resumed. The **Bridge End Inn**, bought by Rowell's in 1932 for £3,716, traded until 1957

when its licence was transferred to the newly-completed **Howlett Hall**, opened on the former Howlett Farm, Denton Burn.

It was the 1960s, a time of extensive demolition and redevelopment, which saw the demise of many Scotswood Rd premises. The **Ordnance**, an Ind Coope house from 1952, and the **Grapes** both closed in 1960. The name **Ordnance** was a word synonymous with Elswick and its workers; when the Crimean War broke out Armstrong turned his attentions to ordnance, inventing breach loading guns and presenting his patents to the government. History records that 'in the first outbreak of indignation and alarm after the disasters of the Crimea the War Office was induced to accept the breach loader, and in 1859 the

The world turned upside down. On Scotswood Rd in 1961 the Freemason's Arms is about to come down as the Cruddas Park flats reach for the sky.

Equality reaches the Green Tree in 1958 as women, as well as their male counterparts, embarked on a journey into space.

for £5,621 in 1923, was rebuilt in the late 1930s and closed in 1962. The **Flax Mill** (once the **Caledonia**) on the corner of Bowman St was a W B Reid house from 1916 and then a Scottish & Newcastle pub before its closure in 1962. Another 1962 casualty was the **Green Tree**, on the junction of Laurel St, with its specially designed corner windows.

Three Newcastle Breweries houses in Scotswood Rd – the **Royal Oak**, the **Maid of Derwent** and the **Bath** – closed in the same week in 1963. In 1892 the **Royal Oak** had 'a spacious bar and two small sitting rooms' on the ground floor and 'a billiard room, club room and small sitting room' on the first floor. A Jas Deuchar property from 1900, it had entrances on Scotswood Rd, Ivy St and Oak St. On the night it closed Bob Richardson, a regular for 40 years, sipped his last pint and mournfully announced that 'Scotswood Road will never the same again'.

The **Maid of Derwent**, a lock-up pub, was sold for £6,900 in 1920 and had become a Jas Deuchar house in the early 1950s. One of the **Bath**'s more celebrated regulars was 'Joe the Horse', a newspaper vendor outside the Central Station and self-styled 'undefeated champion beer-drinker'. Reputed to be able to down 10 pints to his opponent's four, he claimed to have had a medal struck for him by the brewery. Legend has it that defeat finally came in a drinking contest against the wife of a rat-catcher.

The **Gladstone**, on the corner of Clumber St and Scotswood Rd, was acquired by W B Reid in the 1880s and altered and improved in 1932. It closed on the last day of May in 1964 when 'old customers, many of whom are rehoused in other districts, returned to pay their last respects and drowned their sorrows in free beer handed out by manageress, Elizabeth Wood.' One of the regulars who made the sentimental journey was Mrs Wood's father, 77 years old Wm Thomson of Cannon St. It had been 60 years since he had sampled his first beer there.

The **Old Duke of Cumberland**, on the corner of Hare St, was clearly the inspiration for A J Cronin's 'Duke of

Elswick Ordnance Co was established'. Plans for rebuilding the **Ordnance** were drawn up by Arrol's in 1937.

The **Grapes**, on the corner of Hawes St, was bought by the Edinburgh firm of Aitchison's for £4,500 in 1931 and was extensively altered in 1936 when adjoining property was included. By the time it was purchased by the Corporation for £5,260 it had lost much of its local custom through rehousing. Nevertheless, a hundred former regulars crowded into the pub on its last night to hear Lily Dodds, the manageress for 14 years, announce that drinks were on the house.

The **Freemasons' Arms**, on the corner of Tulloch St and known as the **Union Spirit Vaults** until 1883, changed hands

Cumberland, Scottswood Road, Tynecastle' in *The Stars Look Down*. Said to be sited in 'one of the best positions on the busy thoroughfare' and carrying on 'a very large trade', it was rebuilt in 1901. Architectural historian, Lynn Pearson, comments on the design of the architect J Wardle Donald of South Shields who 'emphasised the acute angle of the corner site with a two-storey circular tower which rose from the pub's roof between dormer windows and the chimney-stacks. The top floor of the tower was a single circular room with windows around most of its circumference, which was itself contained in an open-columned drum; the dome was capped by a flèche, and the whole composition made up of one of the most spectacular pubs along a road renowned for them'. The pub's name was shortened to the **Duke of Cumberland** in 1913, it was bought by Newcastle Breweries for £3,500 in 1943 and closed in 1965.

The **Shipwrights Arms** (the **New Burnt House** until the 1920s) was a Cameron's house when it closed in 1965. The **Park Road Hotel** had been renamed the **Clasper Arms** (sometimes **Clasper Hotel**) in memory of the local sporting figure. Harry Clasper, the famous rower, had lived on the site of the pub when it was Armstrong St and later moved into the pub when it was bought with the proceeds of a benefit raised for him. It was purchased by McEwans in 1939 and closed in 1961. The **Rifle**, on the corner of Errington St, was a beerhouse which became a public house with the transference of the licence from the **Weavers' Arms**, Pandon, in 1882. The **Rifle**, bought by W B Reid for £5,000 in 1921, closed in 1966.

Scotswood Rd closures continued into the 1970s. At the **Elswick Hotel**, rebuilt in 1886, Dave Wharton served the last pints in October 1970 to George Robson and Jim Coombe, two old customers with an aggregate 85 years of drinking there. The **Forresters Arms**, a Calder's acquisition from Dover & Newsome Baxter in the first decade of the century, closed in 1971. Its licensed area had been reduced in 1945 when its club room was merged into the residential quarters. At the turn of

The Dene Hotel c.1905. The tramcar on the left is of a type that went out of service in 1908.

the century the **Dene Hotel**, on the corner of Georges Rd, consisted of 'a conveniently and tastefully arranged bar and sitting room' and an upstairs club room with 'division partitions'. Its takings were around £34 per week. The **Dene Hotel** took its name from the nearby Elswick Dene and the one-time Cruddas residence at Dene House. It closed in 1972. Disappearing around the same time was the **Moulders' Arms**, which had been owned by a number of brewing firms, including Morgan's of Norwich, Robert Emmerson's Burton Brewery and Jas Deuchar. A relief manager sent into the **Moulders' Arms** in the 1960s recalls it 'as a terrible place … all the beer was still hand-pumped off the wood, I spent a lot of time stripping down beer engines to ensure they were clean. But it was a lunchtime favourite of office staff from Vickers'.

The Parker's Arms in August 1966. In the background is the shot tower of the Elswick Lead Works, which when completed in 1797 was found to be two feet out of perpendicular. Some of the pub's customers found themselves out of perpendicular on occasions.

Another early 1970s closure was the **Gun** on the corner of Enfield Rd, a former WB Reid house. Its name reflected the reputation Armstrong had as 'the great gunmaker', although it is not clear which particular invention is referred to. One visitor asked 'Was this inn named to commemorate the rifled 3-pounder of 1855, the first of the Armstrong guns? Or was it to honour the 18-pounder which in January 1858, at Shoeburyness, challenged the services' 32-pounder and proved itself a more effective weapon?' For almost two decades from 1938 the landlord of the **Gun** was former boxer, Seaman Tommy Watson, although soon after taking on the pub he was called up by the Royal Navy and his wife, Kathleen, was officially the licensee between 1938 and 1945. His daughter remembered that

'Kitty kept the Gun going for him … it was right opposite the Vicker's ammunition factory, it was a little goldmine. Kitty made a lot of money for him, which he spent freely'. Watson returned to the licensed trade after the war and also resumed his career as a boxing referee. He left the **Gun** to take over the **Blackie Boy** in the Groat Market.

Perhaps because of its landlord's former profession, the **Gun** was regarded as a 'fighters' pub'. One old patron recalled local children congregating at closing time in the hope of witnessing a scrap, but 'to tell the truth, I don't think I ever saw a fight. We'd see men slowly circle each other, and shove each other, but never a blow struck'. The **Gun** is also remembered as 'a rendezvous of the sporting fraternity', when customers included famous boxers and Jack Allen, star of Newcastle United's 1932 Wembley win.

The **Mechanics' Arms**, on the corner of Rendel St, was purchased by A H Higginbottom for £1,300 in 1911 and altered and extended in 1920. It closed in 1977 after a decade of terminal decline during which there was no resident landlord and the premises were systematically vandalised. The **Forge Hammer Inn**, purchased by Duncan & Daglish in 1925 for £5,750, was altered internally in 1952 when the 'off-sales' was removed. Bought by the highways authority in 1985 and initially leased to Drybrough's, the luxuriously tiled pub closed in 1992.

The **Crooked Billet**'s licence was revoked in 1994. The origin of its name has always been the subject of argument and when the matter was raised at the Brewster Sessions of 1916 a lively discussion followed in the columns of a local newspaper. Someone calling himself 'Aad Stamper' repeated the popular view (and common misconception) that the name must derive from its proximity to forges, where iron from furnaces would be beaten into billets. 'I fancy', he wrote, 'that iron and steel rollers – who by occupation as well as nature are a thirsty throng – would resort at this house in the old days'. Unfortunately, the first **Crooked Billet** pre-dates the establishment of the local iron and steelworks. Antiquary Richard Welford's contribution to the debate was to argue that the pub's name was probably rural in character and could refer to 'the pastoral staff, or a baton cornu; a shepherd's crook; the stem of a tree bound up in a faggot, made and sold for fire wood; or from heraldry, being a fesse dancette or a chevron wavy'. Welford also quoted another source concerning woods being cleared of timber 'where scores of roots were taken as crooked billets and for weeks afterwards crooked billets were burned on every cottage fire'. For Welford this is where the solution to the **Crooked Billet**'s name lay. 'What is more natural' he asked, 'than at a time when most people burnt wood and treefelling was common, a man should set up the sign of the crooked billet?'.

Welford's rather lofty view was challenged by another correspondent who recalled the original **Crooked Billet** 'where Armstrong's No 16 Shop is now built beside the Elswick Colliery staithes', and where 'a sign was up and it was a picture of a soldier'. Others suggested that a wayside inn went back to the time of Cromwell, who billetted his troops there on his march from Newcastle to south of Hexham. Whatever the origin of the **Crooked Billet**'s name we can assume it has nothing to do with the obvious answer involving metal-bashing.

In 1896 the **Crooked Billet**, with cocoa rooms and dwelling-house adjoining, went to auction and fetched £15,800. The pub was cited by magistrates' clerk, J R Roberts, when he appeared before Viscount Peel's Licensing Commission. Asked to provide an example of the 'evil of the prolongation of hours during which the long bars are open', Roberts pointed out that the Elswick works employed over 15,000 hands and a pub was situated near the entrance. 'The works open at six o'clock in the morning, and a bell is rung for a few minutes during which the men enter the works. The house is open exactly at six. You will find as many as 50 to 100 men all standing at the door, directly the door is opened they all rush in and their glasses of spirits are all arranged on the counter. They toss off a glass of spirits,

and go straight to their work. At six o'clock in the morning, at the same time these men are going in, the nightshift men come out, and they fill this and other houses in the neighbourhood.'

The last public house on Scotswood Rd (depending on whether we take the earlier or later address of the **King's Head**) was the **Hydraulic Crane**. The pub's name evoked the early years of Armstrong's enterprise when he formed the Newcastle Cranage Co. on Scotswood Rd in 1847. Nicknamed the 'Toll Bar' because it was on the boundary between Elswick and Benwell, it was more recently called **Armstrong's Hydraulic Crane** and the **Armstrong Hotel**. Once the property of the Arthur's Hill Brewery, the pub was acquired by Arrol's and through mergers became a Ind Coope then Tetley's house. It appeared to enjoy a new lease of life with the development of the Newcastle Business Park and plans were drawn up to build

When Robert Deuchar took possession of the Star in 1900 it may well have shone brightly on a dark evening. By the 1950s when this photograph was taken, it was fading fast.

Once a beerhouse, the Druid's Arms was owned by the Ovington Brewery for the first three decades of the century.

changed hands for only £3,750 in 1928 and closed in 1933. The **Crown**, on the corner of Railway St and Ord St, became the **Crown Inn** in c.1938. It was bought by McEwan's in 1926 and closed in the early 1980s to make way for the Redheugh Bridge. The **Globe**, a W B Reid purchase for £4,800 in 1920, still stands.

The **Skiff**, on the corner of Dunn St and Railway St, was bought by W B Reid for £7,800 in 1920, but its licence was only renewed in 1932 on condition that it was cleaned, redecorated and altered. When the **Skiff** closed in 1963 its landlady, Gladys Winter, made a tribute to her regulars. 'The people here are very good. You get none of the trouble which you get in buffets and lounges where toffs quibble about the prices or the time. Here, they go quietly when asked. I always prefer working in the bar, because the working man here is always better than any gentleman'

The **Parker's Arms** in Ord Street, a Hammond's house, closed in 1965. An early closure in Maple St was the **Smiths' Arms** beerhouse in 1887 which became a tinsmith's shop, whilst the **Star** continued until 1966. In Pine St the **Ship Inn** had its licence removed by magistrates in 1892; the **Rector House**, which changed hands for £3,050 in 1915, closed in 1920; Robt Deuchar's **Laburnum Tree** and the **Pineapple**, owned by Tucker's Brewery of Gateshead, lost their licences in 1920.

a hotel at its rear. But following arson attacks and six months in limbo, the former **Hydraulic Crane** was demolished in 1996 on safety grounds.

The streets away from Scotswood Rd also had their fair share of drinking places. In Railway St the **Lord Raglan** and **Prince of Wales** both closed in 1917. The **Locomotive** (once the **Locomotive Engine**) which had been sold for £4,450 in 1896,

Amongst beerhouses to disappear were the **Elswick Tavern**, Elswick St, in 1881; the **Elswick Arms**, Elswick East Terrace, had its licence revoked in 1914; and the **Havelock Arms** (honouring an Indian Mutiny hero who died weeks after the event in 1857), in Elswick Row, closed in 1921 when a Pine Street Brewery property. The **Edinburgh House** in Palace St had a beer and wine only licence, and was owned by Leith distillers, W D Thompson. It had a quoit ground at the rear when it shut up shop in 1906.

In 1883 the **Rock**, on the corner of Park Rd and Cambridge St, was 'in the heart of a populous and respectable locality' and offering 'many attractions to the energetic man of business in search of a sound and valuable investment'. On the ground floor there was a bar, news room, sitting room, office, wholesale store, aerated water manufactory and kitchen. Above was a billiard room, dining room, bedrooms and six attics. As well as a cellar, there was a bottling store, wine store, coachhouse and stable. The **Rock** was acquired by W B Reid in 1921 for £4,600. Plans for its rebuilding were prepared in 1939 but it was not until the 1950s that reconstruction took place. One old resident recalls 'the clever way in which they knocked one half down but kept the other half open, then when they'd half a new pub they opened it and rebuilt the remainder. We eventually got our full pint but you had to do with two halves for a bit.' One Cambridge St drinking place to disappear was the **Cambridge Hotel** in 1920.

Westmorland Road c.1900 with the Villa Victoria in the background. The children are probably more interested in the confectionery shop of John Shotton and the mineral water manufactory of G J Kirkup across the street.

In Sycamore St, on the corner with Laurel St, stood the **Engineers' Arms**. Although the property (consisting of a bar, snug and sitting room, and leased for £80 per annum) was said to be 'well and favourably known in the West End', it closed in 1916. Other premises which closed when trading with beer- or beer and wine-only licence were the **Hare's Nest**, Hare St, in 1875; the **Sir Colin Campbell**, Railway Terrace, in 1876; the **Beethoven**, Sycamore St, in 1883; the **Picnic Inn**, Penn St, when a 'disorderly house' in 1893; the **Golden Lion**, Sycamore St, in 1895 when 'frequented by people for the purpose of betting'; the **Test Inn**, Middle St, when leased by Robt Deuchar for £20 per annum in 1907; and the **Test Tavern**, Brunel St, in 1916. The **Tyneside Hotel**, Water St, was bought by W B Reid in 1899 and closed in 1932.

The Crown around the time of the Coronation. The adjoining premises on Elswick Rd were occupied by builder Henry Bulman, McPherson's hairdressing salon and Graham Leslie the tailor.

1893) closed in 1960.

On Westmorland Rd stands the **Villa Victoria** (originally the **Victoria Cottage**). It was reconstructed in the 1890s, bought by Duncan & Daglish in 1901, and altered in 1931. It did not receive a full publican's licence until 1961. Also still standing on Westmorland Rd is the **Grainger Hotel**, which was altered in 1927, received a full publican's licence in 1958 and was acquired by Hammond's in 1962. The **Cross House**, in Cross Parade, was bought by the Edinburgh firm of Lorimer & Clark in 1935 for £1,700, but plans to rebuild the house were rejected by the justices and it closed in 1936. On Elswick Rd the **Adrian's Head** (once the **Adrianople**) was rebuilt in 1910 and there were alterations in 1961 when one room became a betting shop. In 1983 it became the **Blue Man**, and in 1996 was converted to a hostel.

On what was once Ravensworth View (later Bentinck Rd) but with two doors on Elswick Rd, stood the **Crown** which closed in 1962. The pubs in Elswick were very much 'locals', generally serving the residents of a handful of streets in the immediate vicinity and not doing much evening trade before 8.30 pm. The **Crown**, however, was usually the first public house visited by ex-convicts; being adjacent to the dole office. Released prisoners often made the dole their first port of call and the bar became their next destination.

The **Chesterfield Arms** on the corner of Northbourne St, was bought by W B Reid in 1920 for £7,100 and subsequently became a Scottish & Newcastle Breweries property. In 1990 it was acquired by Legendary Yorkshire Heroes and became the **Independent**, before transferring four years later to Century Inns. In the 1870s the **Dodds Arms**, on the corner of Elswick Rd

In Gloucester St, the **Gloucester Arms** (sometimes the **Gloucester Hotel**) was rebuilt in 1892, bought by Newcastle Hotels Ltd for £4,700 in 1920, taken over by Bass in 1950 and closed in 1962. Also in Gloucester St stood the **Druid's Arms** which was sold for £1,500 in 1933 and then sold on to McEwan's four years later for £3,200. It closed in 1963.

In Tulloch St, the **Tulloch Arms** was being leased by Robt Deuchar for £200 per annum when it closed in 1934, a victim of the magistrates' programme of licence-reduction. In their defence, the owners of the **Tulloch Arms** had unsuccessfully argued that theirs was a special case, being 'the type of house frequented by people preferring comfortable accommodation in moderate sized rooms rather than the noise of the long bar and the large smoke room'. In De Grey St the **Park** (the **Sun** until

and West Parade, had 'a large bar, news room, parlour, two kitchens, two cellars, a long room upstairs, back bedroom and two attics'. It was acquired by Newcastle Breweries 1892 and was rebuilt by the company in 1932. It closed in 1993 when its licence was transferred to the **Groat House** in the city centre.

The **Portland Arms**, originally on Mill Lane, is now effectively on Elswick Rd. Bought by Calder's of Alloa in 1909 it was immediately altered, then in 1939 the magistrates sanctioned the transfer of its licence to a new public house 'to be erected on land occupied by the shop at 3 Mill Lane and properties at 1, 3, and 5 Bentinck St'. The new **Portland Arms** opened for business in 1941.

In Mill Lane the **Park Hotel** lost its licence in 1909; the **Bentinck Arms** closed in 1911; and the **Bentinck Inn** ceased trading in 1922. The **City Hotel** was bought by Duncan & Daglish for £1,800 in 1917, before becoming a Bass house. It was altered in 1934 and 1949, and closed in 1967. The **Belgrave Hotel** (bought along with the **Duke of Gloucester** for £20,000 in 1929) changed hands again for £23,000 in 1950. It became a Hammond's pub in 1962 and closed in 1976.

In Cross Cromwell St the **High Elswick** came near to closure in 1920 but magistrates agreed to renew its licence with a caution as to 'the licensee allowing women to gather together and remain on the premises'. The **High Elswick** fell under the Cromwell Street Compulsory Purchase Order of 1970 and closed in 1972. Also covered by the same order, and closing at the same time, were the **Duke of Gloucester**, Westgate Rd, a Scottish & Newcastle house as a result of its purchase by McEwan's for £9,000 in 1950, and the **Queen's Arms** (formerly the **Queen's Head**), Elswick Row. In Mitford Street the **Tower** was closed in 1917.

As many Elswick pubs closed, two new ones were built on Westmorland Rd. In the Cruddas Park Shopping Centre the **Chieftain** was opened by Newcastle Breweries in 1969. Commemorating the tanks made at Vicker's Elswick works, the two-roomed pub had a distinct military theme: the 842 square feet bar had a photo mural of the interior of a Chieftain tank, and the 1,116 square feet lounge featured the silhouette of a 120mm gun against a brightly camouflaged background as the back fitment to the bar. The **Gold Cup** in Westmorland Rd was opened in 1973 and named after the steeplechase sponsored by Whitbread.

Enjoy the fresh brewed taste of beer from a TANK!

OPEN TONIGHT

THE **CHIEFTAIN**

CRUDDAS PARK NEIGHBOURHOOD CENTRE
Westmorland Road. Elswick. Newcastle

4

Benwell & Scotswood

At the turn of the century, as Benwell was about to be included within the city boundaries, it was said that 'a quarter of a century ago Benwell Village wore an aspect of seclusion and rural peace, but during recent years many of its dwellings have been rebuilt and the new houses have to some degree marred its picturesqueness'. To the old village had been added housing for workmen and the licensed trade quickly expanded their operations to satisfy the thirsts of those who toiled in Benwell's factories and pits.

In old Benwell the **Hawthorn Inn** originally served beer and cider, but its licence was extended in 1897 when taken over by Robt Emmerson of the Burton Brewery, Sandyford. It was bought by Newcastle Hotels Ltd in 1930 and in 1939 the licensing committee approved an application to transfer the licence to a new **Hawthorn Inn** to be erected on the opposite side of the road and extending southwards.

Also in old Benwell, the **Green Tree** was owned by John Dodds of Benwell before its acquisition by Newcastle Breweries. In 1936 the pub was extended and modernised, its floor space being increased from 924 to 4,610 square yards. The owners told the licensing bench that this was necessary because in rush periods there was crowding of customers in passages, yards and outhouses; the increased demand had come from the extensive inter-war housing developments in the neighbourhood. The pub's manager said that trade had increased fivefold during his stewardship and that at times they had as many as two hundred customers on the premises. The **Green Tree**'s licence was revoked by mutual consent in 1997 and demolition began a year later.

The **Benwell House Hotel**, set back on the south side of Benwell Lane, was opened in 1901 in the former Benwell House, built in 1825 as a superior home for John Walker of Wallsend. Purchased in 1901 by Joseph Lamb, owner of the Victoria Hotel in Jarrow, it was converted to public house and carried the nickname 'Lamby's'. The hotel was bought by Rowell's in 1924 for £18,500 and modernised four years later when 'to place public houses on a higher and more refined plane' was 'the laudable endeavour'. The owners applied for a music, singing and dancing licence, but this was restricted to music and singing only after objections from the National British Women's Total Abstinence League. It was also confined to the concert room, but later extended to the balcony so that occasional performances by a small band could be given. This was on the strict understanding that 'no brass or other loud instruments were used and only stringed instruments employed'. A side extension was added to the building in 1937 and the hotel closed in 1969. One manager at the **Benwell House** in the 1960s was particularly impressed by the pub's safe, which was 'a huge cupboard with a steel door where you could go in and do your office work and not be disturbed. Best of all, if you didn't feel like doing the tills last thing at night, you just carried them into the safe and did them the next morning.' The pub was demolished four years after its closure and the Co-operative Funeral Service now occupies part of the site. Some land was given for licensed victuallers' homes and the **Crow's Nest** was built on an area alongside Benwell Lane in 1969.

On the north side of Benwell Lane what was a fine country house, designed by John Dobson for Thomas Crawhall in 1831, was converted to licensed premises in 1978. Benwell Tower, built on the site of the Shafto family seat and incorporating an older tower, has been described as 'one of Dobson's Tudor

Benwell Village in 1903. Those congregating outside the pub are thought to be its landlord, Thos Heslop, with his family and customers.

Surrounded by open fields and alongside a duck pond, the Fox & Hounds of 1900 presents a picture of rural tranquillity.

licensed premises, first as the **Silver Lady** and more appropriately from 1980 as the **Mitre**. The licence was not renewed after 1990 and the building is now the location of television's *Byker Grove*.

The **Benwell Hotel**, on the corner of Adelaide Terrace and Cochrane St, was granted a full licence after its acquisition by Simson & McPherson before the turn of the century. It was altered and extended on the basis of plans drawn up in 1899 by architects Oliver Leeson & Wood. The most obvious change was the impressive new frontage of stone bay windows and parapet. A stone carving on the side of the building is dated 1901. Internally, the pub had bars at the front, a sitting room behind and a room described as a 'private room for the football club'. Upstairs there was a billiard room and a club room. In 1935 further alterations moved a kitchen from the ground floor to the first floor, created a buffet in the space provided and enlarged the bar.

The **Adelaide Hotel** was built on the corner of Elm St and Adelaide Terrace in 1903. The licence was transferred from the about-to-be-demolished **Adelaide** of the early 1970s to a new pub of the same name on the first floor of the Adelaide Shopping Centre. A 1985 directory described it as a 'West End drinking haven' where 'regulars tend to be from an older age

houses, with Tudor-arched openings, many stone mullioned windows and the usual battlements. Inside, a fine staircase, well-proportioned rooms with panelled ceilings and marble chimneypieces'. In 1882 the then owners, the Pease family, gave Benwell Tower to the Newcastle diocese for the Bishop's Palace and a chapel, designed by W S Hicks, was added onto the side. The Bishops of Newcastle resided there until 1943, when the National Fire Service took over the building. From 1946 until 1976 it was the headquarters of Durham & Northumberland Fire and Rescue Brigade and training centre for the Mines Rescue Service. Benwell Tower was then transformed into

group'. This second **Adelaide** had its licence revoked in 1996.

The **Fox & Hounds**, Benwell Bank Top (now the West Rd), originated from at least the beginning of the 19th century and for many years was owned by the Ord then Blackett-Ord families. Until this century the pub had the characteristics of a sleepy country inn. It has been rebuilt and then adapted to changing tastes many times since but has striven to maintain some reference to its rural past: in the mid-1980s, for example, three of its bars were called the Den, the Loft and the Covert Lounge.

The **Fox & Hounds** was bought by Alexander Deuchar in 1931 for £26,777, at the time when new housing was engulfing the area. As the estates spread out further to the western fringes of the city, brewers sought to follow. Arrol's acquired an area of land on the West Rd and applied to construct a public house to be called the

Shortly after opening the Denton Hotel offers 'First Class Accommodation with bed and breakfast for 8s 6d'.

Denton Burn Hotel. There was some local opposition and various claims as to the true expression of public opinion were produced at the brewster sessions of 1936. One objector said he was acting on the instructions of 738 property owners and residents against the proposal, 623 of them living within a quarter-mile radius. This was more than matched by the brewery, which claimed that a 'systematic canvass of the district' had shown 753 persons from within a quarter-mile radius of the site in favour of granting the new licence. Arrol's stressed that their intention was to construct a modern hotel with bedrooms that would be used by motorists, but opponents raised the spectre of 'drink driving' (which was not as fanciful as it may seem when statistics later showed that in 1936 forty-one citizens of Newcastle had been charged with 'being under the influence of drink or drugs whilst in charge of a mechanically-propelled vehicle'). Supporters of the scheme pointed out that the nearest public house to the proposed hotel was the **Fox & Hounds**, 1100 yards away, and argued that 'if a man walked so far he would probably drink more when he got there'.

Permission was granted, but the licensing committee

The Ord Arms during demolition at the end of 1965. In the left foreground work is in progress on an underpass for the new Scotswood Bridge. A sign on the central lamp post points to Scotswood Station.

up for a dining room for resident guests and a lounge for 'ordinary customers' on the first floor. The **Denton** has changed with public tastes over the years: in the early 1970s, for example, it became 'an attractive drive-to-and-eat place with the opening of its new Cavalier Steak bar and lounge'.

At the turn of the century Earl Grey held strong views on the liquor problem, believing that prohibition was not a practical solution and what was required was a system where there was no personal gain to be made from the selling of alcoholic drinks. In 1901 he formed the Northumberland Public House Trust Company to operate licensed premises with the well-being of people at heart and without the profit motive attached to pushing drink sales. This, it was reasoned, would reduce the consumption of alcohol and pubs would become more like refreshment rooms. In 1902 the trust company obtained a licence to build the **Delaval Arms** in Scotswood Rd. Most of the ground floor was taken up by what was described as a 'drawing-room' with a conventional bar at one end and a temperance bar at the other. Other rooms included a dining room seating 150 'where workmen can bring their own bait and have it warmed up, can have the raw material cooked for them, or can purchase from the management's own tariff'. Dinners were to cost between 6d and a shilling. Although Earl Grey's scheme embodied the highest principles, it was run on a very shaky commercial basis. In 1923 the Northumberland Public House

insisted on amendments. For example, the hotel was to be set further back from the road, entrances were to be on the 'projected aerial road', trees were to be planted and dwarf walls built round the grounds. The **Denton Hotel** opened on Race Wednesday in June 1937. After inspecting the new building, the licensing committee publicly acknowledged the skill of the architect and the enterprise of the brewers, expressing the hope that 'instead of tinkering with old premises, other firms would build on similarly enlightened lines'. In 1939 plans were drawn

Trust Co went into liquidation and the **Delaval Arms** was sold to a Scottish brewer, Jas Aitken and then Hammonds in 1962 for £3,450. The pub, which held only a six-day licence before 1963, was still referred to as 'The Trust' until its closure in 1976.

Also on Scotswood Rd, the **Ord Arms** had its own brew-house which operated until the 1870s. Its name evolved from the fact it was owned by the Ord family, later the Blackett-Ords, whose expanses of land to the west and north of Benwell were acquired for housing schemes by the council and private developers between the two world wars. The public house was put up for auction in 1898. This was at the height of a licensed property boom and being near to

The Boat House Inn c.1952 before car crime had been conceived. The only worry for the driver of the soft-drinks delivery van was the reliability of his handbrake.

Scotswood railway station and a new yard being developed by Armstrong-Whitworth, it created much interest from within the trade and also caught the attention of the anti-drink lobby. Rowntree & Sherwell, in their turn of the century work, *The Temperance Problem and Social Reform*, cite the **Ord Arms** as an example of the lengths to which brewers and others would go to secure lucrative licences and acquire the right to rebuild. Rowntree & Sherwell described the house as 'a plain and unpretentious building' which sold for £28,100, a sum 'which the auctioneer acknowledged to be twenty times its value with-

out a licence'. Rowntree & Sherwell also made much of the fact that in the same week the Twizell estate in Northumberland, complete with mansion and seven hundred acres, was sold for less. At that stage the **Ord Arms** consisted of 'bar, parlour, snug, news-room, bagatelle room, kitchen and cellarage' on the ground floor; 'a billiard room, club room and three bed rooms' on the upper floor; 'out-offices comprising a wash house, stabling for six horses and a byre for fourteen cows'; and a 'building occupied as a refreshment room', a yard and a garden of 1,550 square yards.

The unpretentious Mason's Arms in 1950. The original pub had been smaller but in 1900 was extended round the corner when 3 Victoria Terrace was included in the licensed premises.

The **Ord Arms** was bought by F M Laing and rebuilt in 1900, passing via Robt Deuchar in 1937 to Newcastle Breweries in the 1950s. It is fondly remembered for its 'free snacks of cowheel, roast spuds, and tripe'. In December 1965 the **Ord Arms closed** and the next day its manager, Joseph Morgan, walked the few yards to run its replacement, the **Robin Adair**. The **Ord Arms was** demolished but its clock tower was salvaged and placed atop a building at the Tyne Brewery.

The **Robin Adair** took the name of a previous inn on the opposite side of Scotswood Rd immortalised in Geordie Ridley's Tyneside anthem, *The Blaydon Races*, when 'We flew past Armstrong's factory an' up to the Robin Adair'. In the midst of slum clearance programmes Newcastle Breweries expressed the desire to see 'top-class pubs like the Robin Adair rising from the rubble to bring distinction and amenity to out-worn parts of the city'. Officially opened by T Dan Smith, the pub was designed for serious drinkers: at one end there was a bar which could seat 150; another bar where the bar itself stretched the length of the room; a lounge buffet with Japanese and Korean wallpapers and orange curtains; and an off-licence shop. The keynote of the pub's exterior was a panel measuring 16 feet by 10 feet depicting various characters in a horse drawn wagon on their way to Blaydon Races. The mural had 15,000 mosaic pieces and was designed by George Dereford, a Buckinghamshire-based Hungarian whose other work included a coat of arms on the outside of the British Embassy in Tel Aviv. The artist explained that the **Robin Adair** commission took 640 man hours and consisted of antique glass, smalti, ceramic and gold mosaic pieces. He also reassured everyone that the panel would be able to withstand the weather for centuries: quite unnecessary, as it turned out, since less than twenty-five years later the pub was standing disused following a fire. The **Robin Adair** was reported to be in a dilapidated condition and considered to be 'an eyesore and a blemish on the green corridor established on Scotswood Rd'. A Benfield Motors garage now occupies the site.

On the north side of Scotswood Rd, west of Paradise Bridge near to the entrance of the Delavel drift mine, was a row of cottages called Boathouses. At the end of the row stood the **Boat House Inn**, a beerhouse which reverted to an off-licence before its demise in the mid-1960s.

In Scotswood the **Grace Darling**, Denton Rd, served only

beer and cider until a wine licence was added in 1895. It was bought by Rowell's in 1897, altered in 1908, and closed in 1924. Dr Henry Russell, a Lord Mayor of Newcastle, used the former **Grace Darling** building as his first surgery, before moving to Armstrong Rd. The **Masons' Arms** on Prospect Terrace was open from at least the middle of the last century. It had a beer and cider licence, with a wine licence added in 1903. It was bought by Robt Deuchar in 1930 and demolished in 1962.

The **Sporting Arms**, originally restricted to selling beer, was granted an extended licence in 1896 when new premises were built next to the original pub on Denton Rd. In 1901 it was described as 'having a well-fitted bar divided into general, select and family compartments, with three entrances; a smoke room and a kitchen; ample cellarage in the basement; and six rooms on the upper

The Sporting Arms in a photograph taken at the time of the nation's greatest sporting triumph. Is the sporting man on the left quietly shedding a tear as he reflects on the impeccable judgement of Russian linesmen?

floor'. It occupied 'a conspicuous corner site at the junction of five streets'. The **Sporting Arms** was bought by Cameron's for £3,500 in 1922, was extended in 1939 and received a full publican's licence in 1949. In 1957 there were some internal rearrangements which removed the bottle and jug department.

In 1890 the **Rose & Crown**, Chapel Terrace, was a beerhouse with a shop, tap room, snug and 'cellar' on the ground floor, and a three stalled stable in the rear yard. Bought by Bass in 1920 for £2,000, it closed three years later. Also in Chapel Terrace, the **Alma Inn** probably dated from the 1850s when the

Crimean river became famous as the scene of the first battle won by the Allies. The beerhouse received a full licence in 1896 when it was reconstructed largely to the west of its original site. It was acquired by Robt Deuchar for £5,500 in 1946. In 1958 permission was given to transfer the licence to 'new premises to be built on the corner of Armstrong Rd and Ranmere Rd to be know as the Alma'. The old Alma closed in 1961 and was demolished in 1962. The new pub was on Armstrong Rd was actually called the **Bobby Shaftoe**.

Blissfully ignorant of the impending arrival of colourful facia boards, floodlights and advertising, the Alma Inn of the post-war years is hardly distinguishable as a public house.

5

Bell's Close, Lemington, Newburn, Throckley, Walbottle, Westerhope, Cowgate

In 1874 Bell's Close, 3 miles to the west of the city, was described as 'a small village, beautifully situated … noted for its firebrick and lampblack manufactures'. Amongst a small number of licensed premises that had existed in Bell's Close was the **Long Boat Inn**, which did not operate beyond 1860. The **Lamb & Flag** (at times known as **Lamb's Hotel**) had its licence renewed in 1881 on the strict condition that the premises be improved before the next licensing meeting, but the owner decided not to apply for a licence for 1882 and Murray's Stores later occupied the site. The **Rokeby Arms** was run in the middle of the 1850s by Joseph Wren in conjunction with his butchery and grocery business. The property, like much in the area, was originally owned by the Lord Rokebys of Denton Hall who owned the Montague Pit, close to the **Rokeby Arms** and scene of the 1925 disaster. The pub which received a full-licence when it passed to the Marquis of Winchester, was acquired by Northumberland Hotels in 1947 when alterations and additions took place. It was demolished in the late 1980s to make way for the Western Bypass

In Lemington, in an area known as Low Lemington near the Gut, two premises closed around 1880: the **Glasshouse Arms** at the end of High Row and the **Dr Syntax** which became a dwelling house. At South Dissington the **Three Horse Shoes**,

owned by the Duke of Northumberland but run by a Throckley Fell blacksmith, closed in 1874. Its licence was transferred to the **Station Hotel** in Lemington, and the old house pulled down. The **Station Hotel**, on a corner site in Union Hall Rd, was extended in 1926 and again a year after Jas Deuchar bought it in 1947. The pub was often referred to as 'Scotty's'. In the 1980s it fell foul, like many pubs, of the invasion of the pool table when alterations were carried out 'to provide two bars and a separate pool area'. It closed in 1997.

The **Lemington Hotel** at Newburn Hall was owned by the Tyne Brewery Co., then W B Reid, before its licence was cancelled in 1898. It had been used to stable horses for the races on Blaydon Island. A new **Lemington Hotel** in Tyne View was built and became the property of Scottish Brewers in 1959. Its licence was revoked in 1996.

What had been the **Forge Hammer** in the 1860s became the **Tyne Iron Hotel** and was rebuilt in 1937 'on a site adjacent to the LNER and the Lemington Mission Church'. Bought from the trustees of Lord Rokeby by T & J Bernard in 1954, the **Tyne Iron** was known as the 'Hairy Man's'. There are a number of versions as to how it got its nickname, but all refer to the appearance of one of its landlords. The simple explanation is that one of its licensees was particularly hirsute. A more interesting account goes back to the days when the first **Tyne Iron** was situated opposite the Lemington Glassworks and was part of a row of cottages connected with the Tyne Ironworks. The pub was on a lane that ran towards the river and it is said that a seal was washed up near the pub and the landlord arranged for a waistcoat to be made from its skin. The response of customers to his appearance behind the bar wearing his sealskin vest was to bestow upon him the title of 'The Hairy Man'. Bus passengers from Newcastle who frequented the **Tyne Iron** were called 'Hairy's fairies' by residents of Lemington. The **Tyne Iron** became the **New Tyne Iron** in 1990 and closed in 1996.

The old Hairy Man's showing his age in this photograph taken in 1939.

Horseshoes was being run by a local black-smith and it is probably this house which is listed as the **Horseshoe Inn** in 1870 and the **Smiths' Arms** by 1873, before disappearing in the middle of the decade. The **Northumberland Arms** carried on until the end of the century.

In 1895 F M Laing built the **Newburn Hotel** on land purchased from the Duke of Northumberland. The handsome, well-equipped hotel was welcomed by the village, being thought 'a great advantage to commercial men, whilst to holiday makers and those who like a drive from the city, it will be a positive luxury'. The hotel was entered by a spacious hall, after which 'the visitor may find his way into the commercial room, private sitting room, bar parlour, serving counter, and lavatories, all on the same floor. Ascending the broad staircase, there is on the first floor an excellent dining room, a clubroom and a well-fitted billiard room, together with a number of bedrooms. There is also stabling accommodation of an excellent character.' The hotel was bought by Robert Deuchar in 1927 when it was described as 'a modern property of excellent construction in an industrial situation'.

The **Boat** underwent various name changes in the 1880s, going via the **Ferry Boat Inn** and the **Boat House** to the **Boathouse Inn**. The pub is still open in Water Row, although its licence came under threat in 1951 when it was renewed on condition that extensive renovations were carried out. The **Boathouse Inn** was promptly sold by the Duke of Northumberland's estate to Newcastle Breweries and alterations and extensions made. The pub merits a mention in

In the mid-19th century Newburn was feted by the local temperance movement, which reported that 'several warm and energetic advocates had proclaimed teetotal principles to a large meeting of inhabitants'. As a consequence, many confirmed drunkards had 'thrown away the glass' and 'enrolled as soldiers in the cold-water army'. Despite the efforts of the anti-drink activists, Newburn had its dedicated drinkers and directories for the late 1860s show five licensed premises: the **Boat**, the **Highlander Inn**, the **Horseshoe Inn**, the **Smiths' Arms** and the **Northumberland Arms**. An earlier beerhouse, the **Black Boy**, had closed around 1858. The **Highlander** (once the **Highland Laddie**) ceased trading c.1870. In 1852 the **Three**

The Northumberland Arms sometime during John Gunn's ten-year stewardship from 1881. The licensee and his family appear to be serving local workmen.

The Engine Inn c.1952, shortly after its acquisition by W.B. Reid. The delivery van belongs to James Wright, a baker on the West Rd.

cottages, to be called Heddon Square, was erected as miners' homes in 1796 by Messrs Bells & Brown of the Heddon Colliery. As the houses were being completed three-hundred French Royalist clergymen arrived in Newcastle; they had originally fled the Revolution by moving to the Channel Isles from where the British authorities directed them to Northumberland. The nine cottages intended for Heddon miners were allocated to 38 French refugees. In 1802, after the Peace of Amiens, the clergymen returned home but Heddon Square had become known as Frenchman's Row. The end house on the row was used by the French as a beerhouse and was christened the **Royal French Arms**. It was rebuilt in brick as an inn and received a full licence in 1899. In mid-summer 1998 the building was boarded up, giving no clue to its identity as a historic public house.

In Walbottle in the 1850s a farmer ran the **Percy Arms** As its name suggests, the property was owned by the Duke of Northumberland and the pub remained a free house (as the fully-licensed **Percy Arms Hotel**) until bought by Newcastle Breweries in 1943. In 1961 a pre-fabricated betting office was sited there, the result of a recent act which liberalised gambling, made an army of bookies' runners redundant and saw nearly 14,000 betting shops spring up in Britain within twelve months.

The other Walbottle licensed premises owned by the House of Percy were the **Brown Jug**, the **Half Moon**, the **White Swan**

Pevsner's *Buildings of Northumberland* as 'a pleasant stone house of c.1830; the quoins are marked with the levels of the floods of 1771, 1815, 1830 and 1856.' Scottish & Newcastle disposed of the **Boathouse Inn** to private owners in 1987. Newburn acquired a new public house in 1996 when the converted pumping station of 1854 was opened as the **Keelman** by the Big Lamp Brewery, which was transforming the rest of the buildings into new brewing facilities.

On the city boundary with Heddon a row of brown-stone

Harvest time in Cowgate. The original Mill Inn when John Smart was licensee in 1902.

and the **Engine**. The **Brown Jug** and the **Half Moon** did not survive beyond the 1860s. The **White Swan** at Loughbridge surrendered its licence in 1880. The **Engine**'s name is probably explained by its position close to colliery workings and an incline which may well have housed a stationary engine. It became the **Locomotive Inn** in 1870s and in 1907 a removal order was granted to a new building adjoining the original premises. It reverted to being the Engine **Inn** once more and was acquired by W B Reid from the Duke of Northumberland in 1948, then Scottish Brewers in 1959. It became the **Original Masons** in 1991.

At the end of the last century, Throckley enjoyed a reputation in temperance circles as one of the north's 'dry villages'. The National Prohibition Convention of 1897 was told that Alderman W H Stephenson, who owned the colliery company which leased the estate, prohibited the liquor traffic 'because he is thoroughly convinced the inhabitants wish it'. The convention's handbook explained that 'formerly there were two public houses' but now 'not only can the inhabitants not buy drink, but they may not keep dogs or pigeons, and gamble on the result of rabbit-coursing, greyhound-racing or pigeon-flying'. A glowing picture was painted of life in the village, where 'half of the miners are total abstainers, for the prohibition of drink, dogs, and pigeons keeps away those that are inclined thereto, and the result of the repulsion of these free-livers is a sort of artificial selection of steady workmen, who have in the course of years formed themselves into an industrious, peaceable and thriving community'. The ministers and clergy reported that 'the numbers of men attending morning service at places of worship is quite exceptional'. The miners were also 'equally good in turning up for work in an efficient condition on Monday mornings, guiltless of "after-damp" from any Saturday or Sunday potations' .

The residents of Throckley were eventually given the opportunity to drink on their own patch in 1908, when a working-men's club was opened on land owned by a local garage proprietor. Some 42 years later Newcastle Breweries obtained a provisional licence for a public house to be built on the Mount Pleasant estate. This eventually materialised as the **Centurion** which became the **Throckley Inn** in 1984, then the **Centurion** again when acquired by Go Ahead Leisure 1990.

Before Wade's 1751 turnpike (now known as the Military Road) was built on the line of the Roman Wall, the road to Carlisle ran via Cowgate where there was a well-used inn. At the time of the First World War Cowgate was still a rural area, its only landmarks being its inns and windmill. The **Windmill Inn** (previously the **Mill Inn**) had only a beer and cider licence when owned by the Fenham Estates in 1903. By 1934, however, it had developed into 'a big, handsome establishment'. It was a Vaux house when it closed in 1996 and was later demolished. On the tithe maps of 1841 Wm Ord is shown as owning the **Cowgate Inn** and land, and it would seem that the inn adopted the family name to become the **Ord Arms** not long after. The Ords were very prominent land-owners, residing in Fenham Hall between 1695 and 1835, and giving their name to a number of public houses. Wm Ord entered Parliament at the age of 21; one obituary pays fulsome tribute to the way in which he 'assisted in abolishing the abominable slave trade, and in extirpating slavery itself from those dominions; in repealing the Test and Corporation Acts; and in emancipating our Roman Catholic Countrymen'. When he died in 1855 Wm Ord was the last male descendant and the valuable estates passed to a son of the Rev J A Blackett of Wolsingham, who had married a niece of Ord.

The **Ord Arms** was altered in 1900 and in 1930 Alexander Deuchar purchased the premises outright and prepared plans for rebuilding. Licensing magistrates were told that 'until recently the Ord Arms was a wayside hostelry, but with the growth of the Cowgate estate abnormal demands were being made on the accommodation. Queues are frequent and the

The Jingling Gate c.1910. The main structure of the pub remains unchanged, despite the many modifications over the years, the mock-tudor camouflage, and the now almost obligatory conservatory.

place is often crowded'. The pub was taken over from S & N by Camerons in 1996 and at the time of writing is closed.

The **Jingling Gate Inn may** have originally been called the **Blue Bell** and certainly began with its current name spelt **Gingling Gate**. It was acquired from the Duke of Northumberland by North Eastern Breweries and in 1906 its licence was renewed on condition that alterations were carried out. The **Jingling Gate** was remodelled in the mid-1930s and extended by Vaux in 1958.

6

Some Post-War Developments

In 1938 Alexander Deuchar applied for what was called a 'provisional ordinary removal' which would allow him to close the **Westmorland Hotel**, Westmorland Rd, and build the **Fenham Hotel** in Silver Lonnen. War intervened and a barrage balloon hung in the sky above Silver Lonnen, but when peace came war-weary locals were promised a public house on the vacant site. Post-war restrictions, lack of materials and labour shortages delayed the arrival of what had initially been referred to as the proposed **Fenham Hotel**. In 1952 the licensing justices granted an application for premises intended to be known as the **Silver Lonnen**, but the pub opened in 1954 under the sign of the **Balloon** as the brewery acknowledged the popular name by which locals called the scheme. When the **Balloon** finally went up it was only as a temporary, breeze-block structure, and was replaced by a new version built next door nine years later. The new **Balloon** had three public rooms, including a bar which was 'very masculine but comfortably furnished' and a buffet with a 'comfortable, masculine air' but somehow managed 'to combine perfectly the requirements of both males and females'. The present sign on the **Balloon** ignores the origins of the pub's name and represents a balloon more akin to one designed by the Montgolfier brothers than one intended to foil the Luftwaffe.

On Stamfordham Rd the **Rokeby** opened in 1952 with a licence previously attached to the **King Edward** in Bath Lane. Occupying a former wartime Ministry of Defence building which had housed an army radar post, it developed into both a landmark and eyesore. In 1995 Cameron's demolished the **Rokeby** and rebuilt it at a cost of £750, 000. Thankfully and perhaps unusually, the brewery gave some thought to the new pub's name; they recognised the historic links to the locality of the old pub's name and also reflected the superiority of the replacement premises by calling it the **Lord Rokeby**. The building was not, however, entirely original; the single storey design with multi-level roofs was based on a Hartlepool pub called the Greensides.

As post-war restrictions were relaxed new public houses began to spring up in the areas of new housing developments. A provisional licence was granted for a pub on the Newbiggin Hall estate which was going up on the site of Newbiggin Hall, an early 19th century replacement of an older house. When the licence was confirmed in 1960 a staircase from the hall was incorporated into the pub which, by error or for some more obscure reason, was called the **Newbiggen Hall Hotel**, with the penultimate letter of the first word of its name differing from that of the old hall and the new estate. Once opened, the pub became the focal point for the estate in many ways: it was not until 1967 that residents' efforts ensured the construction of a church and in the early 1960s religious services were held in the **Newbiggen Hall Hotel**. The church continues to function but the pub has disappeared following a fire.

Modern pubs appeared on modern estates, but the male-dominated culture of the old public house was still evident. When opening the **Hillheads**, in Westerhope in 1962, the owners declared that 'the men of the North East have always been good judges of beer – and in this affluent age they like it in surroundings which, if not the last word in luxury, are tastefully and comfortably furnished'. A year later saw the opening of the new **Runnymede**, with its 'modern simplicity of line planned to conform to the general scheme of development in the district'. There was a 60ft lounge, a buffet and a bar designed to be 'a real man's room'.

The new **Runnymede** was built alongside its predecessor, an older **Runnymede** which had received a provisional licence in 1947. A temporary conversion from a Victorian dwelling during the post-war era of building restrictions, the old house had an interesting history. It was constructed by Joseph W Wakinshaw, a man whose obituary pointed out that 'his great life-work was developing garden cities, bringing people back to the land, and no other man in England has done so much in this direction. Before places like Letchworth were thought of he was planning Westerhope, Cleadon, Whickham and Stocksfield, to be followed by Rowlands Gill, Darras Hall, Stockton Grange, Shotley Bridge, Axwell Park and Otterburn Hall'. Wakinshaw had formed the Northern Allotment Society in 1890 and twelve months later suggested that the society's members combine to purchase land which they could sub-divide into plots for houses and small-holdings. They bought 61 acres of Red Cow Farm, situated in what was then referred to as East Denton, and a number of houses, including Runnymede, were built. With a name required for the hamlet, Red Cow was put forward but it was a name dreamed up by Robert Hisco which stood the test of time. Hisco's son, Ralph, revealed how his father thought that Red Cow was 'not particularly euphonious as a village name … He suggested Westerhope … because the estate was situated west of Newcastle and also they were going into the country with a sense of hope'. So it was that the sign on the public house and the district where it stood had their origins in the efforts of a handful of late 19th century idealists. The introduction of a public house had been a controversial move, since the original Red Cow Estate committee had included a restrictive 'no alehouses' covenant in their agreement. Before his death in 1938, Robert Hisco had helped uphold the covenant ruling when it was suggested that a pub should be built. In 1947, however, householders voted to relax the covenant and allow a pub in the house of the late Rev. Wakenshaw, a temperance advocate and brother of J W Wakenshaw. Unfortunately

A painful echo of the sixties. The Hillheads alive with the sound of muzak.

the name Runnymede was extinguished in 1997 when the pub became the **New Inn**.

Amongst other arrivals in the 1960s was the **Peregrine**, West Denton, which opened in 1964. Permission to build the pub was given as early as 1947 when the licensing magistrates granted Newcastle Breweries a provisional removal from the Bird Inn, Wylam.

For some the 1960s was the 'age of Aquarius', but for brewers it was the 'age of Formica'. The **Runnymede**'s bar contained tables with Formica tops, the buffet had panels of grey and black Formica on its bar and the lounge's counter was 'padded with alternating panels of black and moss green plastic material with Formica verticals introduced at wide intervals'. Similarly, advertising features for the **Balloon** spoke of the bar-

Owen Brannigan opens the Cushy Butterfield in 1968 watched by the licensee, Alice Walker who was previously at the Globe in Railway St and before that at the Crown.

room's 'Formica-topped tables' and 'Formica-topped bar', whilst the feature of the buffet was its 'vynide padded Formica-topped bar'. The service counter in the **Peregrine**'s buffet had 'a patterned Formica top' and armchairs in the lounge enabled 'cosy groups to be formed around the Formica topped tables'.

In 1966 the **Turnpike** was opened at Chapel House. To most people the flat-roofed brick-built pub would appear unremarkable, but to Bass it was a 'luxurious and well-appointed wining and dining centre'. A new word was introduced to the local licensed trade: one of the main features of the public house was to be a 'dinette'. In 1968 the **Cushy Butterfield**, just off Scotswood Rd in Sanderson St, became (after the **Robin Adair**) 'the second of a new generation of licensed houses far removed

from the grimy drinking places which once stood on almost every corner of the long, straight road that leads to Blaydon'. Opened by Owen Brannigan, who provided a rendition of the obvious ditty, the pub closed within fifteen years. Many customers were lost when housing in the neighbourhood was demolished and the **Cushy Butterfield** stood vandalised and damaged for a few years until pulled down in the mid-1980s.

New, if uninspiring, public houses continued to appear in the 1970s: for example, the **Whin Dyke** in Denton Park Shopping Centre in 1970, the **Vallum** on the Dumpling Hall estate in 1972 and **Chapel Park** on the development of the same name in 1973. The way public houses were to evolve into the 1980s and beyond can be gleaned from the **Howlett Hall**, Denton Burn, which in 1985 was described as 'an estate pub' which had 'facilities for pool, darts, dominoes … a juke box, fruit machines and television, and live entertainment every Thursday night'. Since the war public houses have undergone invasion from the latest fad or piece of equipment as, for example, the 1950s novelty of background muzak and monochrome televisions have given way to loud music and giant screens. Almost forty years ago the *Evening Chronicle* warned that 'the peace and quiet of many a local are being shattered. And the culprit is the juke-box'. In pointing out that customers may well 'have to drink to the outpourings of Cliff Richard', the newspaper provided a most horrific hint of how pubs might develop. Sadly, nobody appeared to take heed.

INDEX